Copyright © 2024 by Rachael Akinpelu

All rights reserved.

No part of this publication may be reproduced, distributed, or transmitted in any form or by any means, including photocopying, recording, or other electronic or mechanical methods, without the prior written permission of the publisher.

Published by The Authorpreneur Hub

All inquiries should be directed to
rachaelakinpelu01@gmail.com

May the pages of this book be a constant reminder that God loves you and made you for a purpose.

I am loved by God and I am wonderfully made!

It's amazing how
much love God has for me.
I see it all around!

He made the sun to brighten my day.

The moon and stars to give light at night time.

He made the sky, the clouds, and the rain to help our plants grow.

He made the birds that fly so high.

He made the sea
and all the beautiful
animals in it.
The whales, the sharks,
and the little fish.

He made the earth and the trees to give us nourishment.

God loves me so much;
He gave me
Mommy and Daddy
to love and care for me.

He gave me friends,
to laugh and play
and make our
hearts joyful.

I am loved,
I am valuable
and uniquely made!

God's love for me
never ends.
He gave his son,
Jesus for me
Thank you, God,
for loving me
and making me special!

Bible Verses

Genesis 1:1

In the beginning God created the heaven and the earth.

1 John 4:19

We love him, because he first loved us.

I John 4:8

He who does not love does not know God, for God is love.

John 3:16

For God so loved the world that He gave His only begotten Son, that whoever believes in Him should not perish but have everlasting life.

Philippians 4:13

I can do all things through Christ who strengthens me.

Bible Verses

Psalms 150:6

Let everything that has breath praise the Lord. Praise the Lord!

Philippians 4:4

Rejoice in the Lord always. Again I will say, rejoice!

Romans 10:13

For "whoever calls on the name of the Lord shall be saved."

Psalms 23:1

The Lord is my shepherd; I shall not want.

Romans 8:37

Yet in all these things we are more than conquerors through Him who loved us.

Milton Keynes UK
Ingram Content Group UK Ltd.
UKHW051835151124
451187UK00009B/100

9 781069 141804